GOD'S

Promises
for
Your Senior Years

Harold and Luci Shaw

A Meridian Publication
Grand Rapids, Michigan
Manufactured in the United States of America.

GOD'S
Promises
for
Your Senior Years

Presented to

_____

_____

_____

GOD'S
Promises *for* Your Senior Years

Is dedicated to

its creators
Hal and Luci Shaw

and to my own parents
who in their senior years,
while not always golden,
found comfort in
God's Promises.

— The Publisher

This book is published by special arrangement with
Harold Shaw Publishers,
Box 567, Wheaton, Illinois 60189.

Copyright 1983 by Harold Shaw Publishers,
Created by Harold and Luci Shaw

Published by HSP as Promises for the Senior Years.

Where the King James Version (KJV) is used, antiquated words
(such as "shouldst") have been replaced with contemporary words
(like "should").

Grateful acknowledgment is made to the publishers of the Scripture
versions, portions of which are quoted in this book, using the
following abbreviations:

KJV: The King James Version

NRSV: New Revised Standard Version

NIV: The New International Version

NKJV: The New King James Version

Phillips: The New Testament In Modern English by J.B. Phillips

RSV: The Revised Standard Version

NASB: New American Standard Bible

TEV: Today's English Version (Good News Bible)

TLB: The Living Bible

GW: God's Word

The Holy Bible, New International Version, Copyright 1978 by
New York International Bible Society. Used by permission.

The Holy Bible, New King James Version, Copyright 1979, 1980, 1982
by Thomas Nelson, Inc. Used by permission

The New Testament in Modern English, revised edition by
J.B. Phillips. Used by permission of the Macmillan Publishing
Company, Inc.

Promises for the Senior Years was initially compiled by Ann K. Alexander and Jean Hooten of Harold Shaw Publishers, and for this edition expanded and edited by Rebecca Humm of Meridian Publications.

M018X Medallion Paperback

1-56570-018-X

Cover and book design by Joel A Jetzer

Meridian Publications
Grand Rapids, Michigan 49546
meridian@omco.com

Manufactured in the United States of America.

Contents

God Cares About Me   11

God Gives Purpose to My Life   35

God Makes Me Feel Secure   57

When I Am Hurting   73

My Family   101

Hope of Heaven   133

God Cares About Me

I Am God's Child
God Cares
God Sustains
God Hears My Prayers
The Lord is in Control
I Am Important to God
God Keeps His Promises
God Wants Me
God Forgives Me
God Is Real
The Lord is Changeless
God Loves Me
God Is Fair

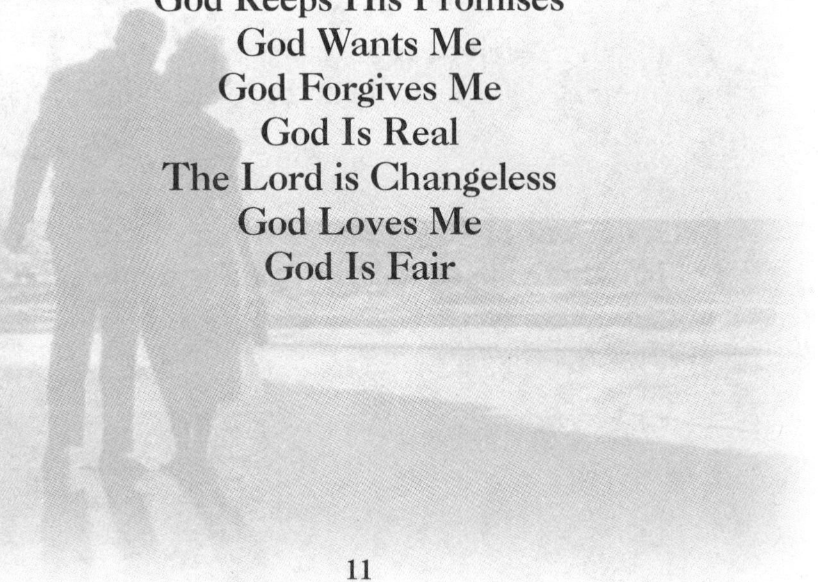

I Am God's Child

God is so awesome and I feel insignificant.
How can I know him as a close, loving Father
and personal friend?

You shall seek me, and find me, when you shall
search for me with all your heart. And I will be
found of you, says the Lord.

Jeremiah 29:13-14 KJV

To all who received him, who believed in
his name, he gave power to become children
of God.

John 1:12 RSV

Even to your old age and gray hairs I am he, I
am he who will sustain you. I have made you
and I will carry you; I will sustain you and I
will rescue you.

Isaiah 46:4 NIV

He is like a father to us, tender and sympathetic
to those who reverence him.

Psalm 103:13 TLB

His Holy Spirit speaks to us deep in our hearts,
and tells us that we really are God's children.

Romans 8:16 TLB

O Lord my God, many and many a time you
have done great miracles for us, and we are
ever in your thoughts.

Psalm 40:5 TLB

God Cares

*Selfishness, suffering, and evil abound
in this world. Is there a
caring God in the midst of all this?*

This is how God showed his love among us: He
sent his one and only Son into the world that we
might live through him.

1 John 4:9 NIV

You will listen, O Lord, to the prayers of the lowly; you will give them courage. You will hear the cries of the oppressed and the orphans; you will judge in their favor, so that mortal men may cause terror no more.

Psalm 10:17-18 TEV

This plan of mine is not what you would work out, neither are my thoughts the same as yours! For just as the heavens are higher than the earth, so are my ways higher than yours, and my thoughts than yours.

Isaiah 55:8-9 TLB

Know therefore that the Lord your God is God; he is the faithful God, keeping his covenant of love to a thousand generations of those who love him and keep his commands.

Deuteronomy 7:9 NIV

He has not despised or disdained the suffering of the afflicted one; he has not hidden his face from his but has listened to his cry for help.

Psalm 22:24 NIV

The mountains may depart and the hills be removed, but my steadfast love shall not depart from you, and my covenant of peace shall not be removed, says the Lord, who has compassion on you.

Isaiah 54:10 RSV

The Lord longs to be gracious to you; he rises to show you compassion. For the Lord is a God of justice. Blessed are all who wait for him!

Isaiah 30:18 NIV

Blessed be the God and Father of our Lord Jesus Christ, the Father of mercies and God of all comfort, who comforts us in all our affliction, so that we may be able to comfort those who are in any affliction, with the comfort with which we ourselves are comforted by God. For as we share abundantly in Christ's sufferings, so through Christ we share abundantly in comfort too.

2 Corinthians 1:3-5 RSV

We know that all things work together for good to them that love God, to them who are called according to his purpose.

Romans 8:28 KJV

Little children, you are God's family, and you have won a victory over these people, because He who is in you is greater than he who is in the world.

I John 4:4 GW

God Sustains

God seems so far away. Is he really active today? Does he make a difference in the world?

The Lord your God is he that goes with you, to fight for you against your enemies, to save you.

Deuteronomy 20:4 KJV

We know that all things work together for good
to them that love God, to them who are the
called according to his purpose.   *Romans 8:28 KJV*

Jesus Christ the same yesterday, and today,
and forever.   *Hebrews 13:8 KJV*

God Hears My Prayers
*Sometimes it is hard to feel that God
is listening when I pray. How can I know
that God hears my prayers?*

The righteous cry, and the Lord hears, and
delivers them out of all their troubles.
          Psalm 34:17 KJV

You will call upon me and come and pray to me, and I will listen to you. You will seek me and find me when you seek me with all your heart.

Jeremiah 29:12-13 NIV

I am the Lord, who exercises kindness, justice and righteousness on earth, for in these I delight.

Jeremiah 9:24 NIV

This is the confidence that we have in him, that, if we ask anything according to his will, he hears us: And if we know that he hears us, whatsoever we ask, we know that we have the petitions that we desired of him.

1 John 5:14-15 KJV

Whatever you ask for in prayer with faith, you will receive.

Matthew 21:22 NRSV

The effectual fervent prayer of a righteous man avails much.

James 5:16 KJV

Again, truly I tell you, if two of you agree on earth about anything you ask, it will be done for you by my Father in heaven.

Matthew 18:19 NRSV

Ask, and it shall be given you; seek, and you shall find; knock, and it shall be opened unto you: for everyone that asks, receives; and he that seeks, finds; and to him that knocks, it shall be opened.

Matthew 7: 7-8 KJV

Very truly, I tell you, if you ask anything of the Father in my name, he will give it to you.

John 16:23 NRSV

So I say to you, Ask, and it will be given you; search, and you will find; knock, and the door will be opened for you. For everyone who asks receives, and everyone who searches finds, and for everyone who knocks, the door will be opened.

Luke 11: 9-10 NRSV

The Lord is in Control

*Many things happen over which I have no
control. How can I know that
God is still in control?*

The Lord is still in his holy temple; he still rules
from heaven. He closely watches everything
that happens here on earth.

Psalm 11:4 TLB

God shall bring every work into judgment, with
every secret thing, whether it be good, or
whether it be evil.

Ecclesiastes 12:14 KJV

Oh Lord God! Behold, you have made the
heaven and the earth by your great power and
stretched out arm, and there is nothing too hard
for you... Behold, I am the Lord, the God of all
flesh: is there anything too hard for me?

Jeremiah 32:17,27 KJV

Yours, O Lord, is the greatness and the power and the glory and the majesty and the splendor, for everything in heaven and earth is yours. Yours, O Lord, is the kingdom; you are exalted as head over all. Wealth and honor come from you; you are the ruler of all things. In your hands are strength and power to exalt and give strength to all.

1 Chronicles 29:11-12 NIV

Even to your old age and gray hairs I am he, I am he who will sustain you. I have made you and I will carry you; I will sustain you and I will rescue you.

Isaiah 46:4 NIV

Jesus Christ the same yesterday, and today, and forever.

Hebrews 13:8 KJV

The Lord your God is he that goes with you, to fight for you against your enemies, to save you.

Deuteronomy 20:4 KJV

This plan of mine is not what you would work out; neither are my thoughts the same as yours! For just as the heavens are higher than the earth, so are my ways higher than yours, and my thoughts than yours.

Isaiah 55:8-9 TLB

I am the Lord, I change not.

Malachi 3:6 KJV

I Am Important to God
*Even my big problems are probably
very small to the Creator of the universe.
Does God really care about the
details of my life?*

I am poor and needy; yet the Lord thinks upon me: you are my help and my deliverer.

Psalm 40:17 KJV

Let him have all your worries and cares, for he is always thinking about you and watching everything that concerns you.

1 Peter 5:7 TLB

Fear not: for I have redeemed you, I have called you by your name; you are mine.

Isaiah 43:1 KJV

Are not two sparrows sold for a penny? Yet not one of them will fall to the ground apart from your Father. And even the hairs of your head are all counted.

Matthew 10:29-30 NRSV

How precious it is, Lord, to realize that you are thinking about me constantly! I can't even count how many times a day your thoughts turn toward me. And when I waken in the morning, you are still thinking of me!

Psalm 139:17-18 TLB

Neither height, nor depth, nor anything else in all creation, will be able to separate us from the love of God that is in Christ Jesus our Lord.

Romans 8:39 NIV

God Keeps His Promises
When life seems overwhelming and it looks as if God isn't keeping his promises, how can I feel assured of his faithfulness?

Let us hold on firmly to the hope we profess, because we can trust God to keep his promise.

Hebrews 10:23 TEV

No matter how may promises God has made, they are "Yes" in Christ.

2 Corinthians 1:20 NIV

The God who made both earth and heaven, the seas and everything in them—he is the God who keeps every promise.

Psalm 146:6 TLB

His divine power has given us everything needed for life and godliness, through the knowledge of him who called us by his own glory and goodness. Thus he has given us, through these things, his precious and very great promises, so that through them you may escape from the corruption that is in the world because of lust, and may become participants of the divine nature.

2 Peter 1:3-4 NRSV

God Wants Me

I have never given much thought to God. Can I turn to him now, when life seems to be closing in on me?

God so loved the world that he gave his only Son, that whoever believes in him should not perish but have eternal life. For God sent the Son into the world, not to condemn the world, but that the world might be saved through him.

John 3:16-17 RSV

He is patient with you, not wanting anyone to perish, but everyone to come to repentance.

2 Peter 3:9 NIV

Repent, then, and turn to God, so that your sins may be wiped out, that times of refreshing may come from the Lord.

Acts 3:19 NIV

This is what love is: it is not that we have loved God, but that he loved us and sent his Son to be the means by which our sins are forgiven.

1 John 4:10 TEV

God Forgives Me

I have lived carelessly most of my life. Are my sins too many or too terrible for God to forgive?

For there is not a just man upon earth, that does good, and sins not.

Ecclesiastes 7:20 KJV

Listen! In this man Jesus, there is forgiveness for your sins! Everyone who trusts in him is freed from all guilt and declared righteous.

Acts 13:38-39 TLB

You are a forgiving God, gracious and compassionate, slow to anger and abounding in love.

Nehemiah 9:17 NIV

Let the wicked forsake his way, and the unrighteous man his thoughts: and let him return unto the Lord, and he will have mercy upon him; and to our God, for he will abundantly pardon.

Isaiah 55:7 KJV

If we confess our sins, he is faithful and just to forgive us our sins and to cleanse us from all unrighteousness.

I John 1:9 KJV

Then I acknowledged my sin to you, and I did not hide my iniquity; I said, " I will confess my transgressions to the Lord," and you forgave the guilt of my sin.

Psalm 32:5 NRSV

O Lord, you are so good and kind, so ready to forgive; so full of mercy for all who ask your aid.

Psalm 86:5 TLB

Repent, then, and turn to God, so that your sins may be wiped out, the times of refreshing may come from the Lord.

Acts 3:19 NIV

As far as the east is from the west, so far has he removed our transgressions from us.

Psalm 103:12 NASB

God Is Real

*Some of the things I read and hear
present opposing views of God.
How can I know who he really is?*

If you continue in my word, then are you my
disciples indeed; and you shall know the truth,
and the truth shall make you free.

John 8:31-32 KJV

I will bring the blind by a way that they knew
not; I will lead them in paths that they have not
known: I will make darkness light before them,
and crooked things straight. These things will I
do unto them, and not forsake them.

Isaiah 42:16 KJV

The entrance of your words gives light.

Psalm 119:130 NIV

You shall guide me with your counsel, and afterward receive me to glory.

Psalm 73:24 KJV

The Lord is Changeless
Everything around me is changing.
Will God stay the same?

I am the Lord, I change not.

Malachi 3:6 KJV

Jesus Christ the same yesterday, and today, and forever.

Hebrews 13:8 KJV

Before you created the hills or brought the world into being, you were eternally God, and will be God forever.

Psalm 90:2 TEV

Every good and perfect gift is from above, coming down from the Father of the heavenly lights, who does not change like shifting shadows.

James 1:17 NIV

God Loves Me

*When I go through dry periods in my
spiritual life or times of struggle, how can
I know God still loves me?*

I have loved you with an everlasting love: therefore with lovingkindness have I drawn you.

Jeremiah 31:3 KJV

God demonstrates his own love for us in this:
While we were still sinners, Christ died for us.

Romans 5:8 NIV

As the Father has loved me, so have I loved
you. Now remain in my love.

John 15:9 NIV

The Lord is merciful and loving, slow to become
angry and full of constant love.

Psalm 103:8 TEV

You are precious to me and honored, and I
love you.

Isaiah 43:4 TLB

Know therefore that the Lord your God is God;
he is the faithful God, keeping his covenant of
love to a thousand generations of those who
love him and keep his commands.

Deuteronomy 7:9 NIV

This is how God showed his love among us: He
sent his one and only Son in the world that we
might live through him. This is love: not that we
loved God, but that he loved us and sent his
Son as an atoning sacrifice for our sins.

I John 4:9-10 NIV

God is Fair

It frustrates me to see bad things
happen to good people. How can
I know that God is fair?

"I am the Lord, who exercises kindness, justice
and righteousness on earth, for in these I delight."

Jeremiah 9:24 NIV

God shall bring every work into judgment, with
every secret thing, whether it be good, or
whether it be evil.

Ecclesiastes 12:14 KJV

The Lord is just in all his ways, and kind in all
his doings. The Lord is near to all who call
upon him, to all who call upon him in truth.

Psalm 145:17-18 RSV

The mountains shall depart, and the hills be removed; but my kindness shall not depart from you, neither shall the covenant of my peace be removed, says the Lord that has mercy on you.

Isaiah 54:10 KJV

God Gives Purpose To My Life

I Am Special to God
I Can Honor God
God Remains Faithful
God Forgives
God Gives My Life Purpose
God's Goal for My Life
I Can Serve God
God Is Always With Me
God Helps Me Grow
God Speaks to Me

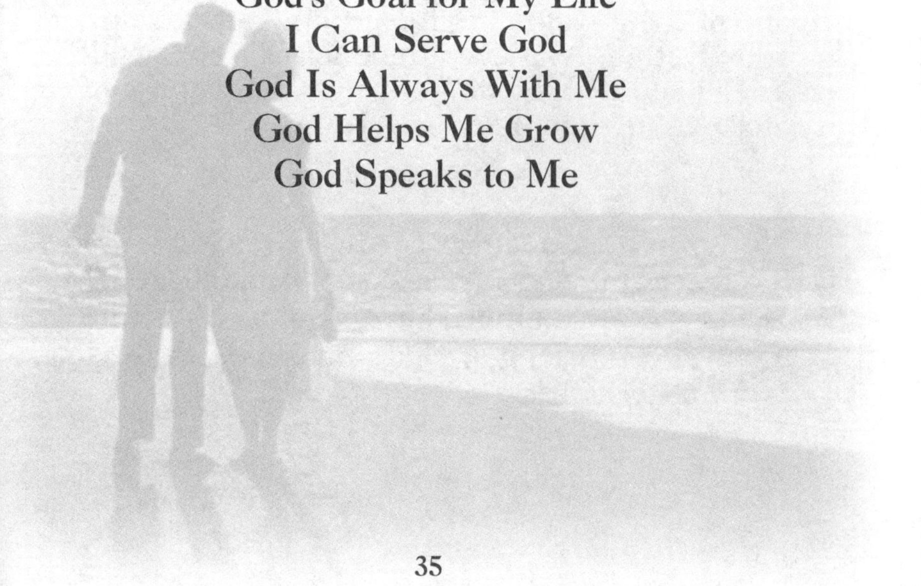

I Am Special to God

Sometimes I don't feel good about myself.
Am I of value to God?

God created man in his own image, in the
image of God created he him; male and female
created he them.

Genesis 1:27 KJV

Are not two sparrows sold for a penny? Yet not
one of them will fall to the ground apart from
your Father. And even the hairs of your head
are all counted. So do not be afraid; you are of
more value than many sparrows.

Matthew 10:29-31 NRSV

Now you are no longer strangers to God and
foreigners to heaven, but you are members of
God's very own family, citizens of God's coun-
try, and you belong in God's household with
every other Christian.

Ephesians 2:19 TLB

You are precious to me and honored, and I
love you.

Isaiah 43:3 TLB

Behold, what manner of love the Father has
bestowed upon us, that we should be called the
sons of God.

1 John 3:1 KJV

Yes, I have loved you with an everlasting love:
therefore with lovingkindness have I
drawn you.

Jeremiah 31:3 KJV

I Can Honor God
How can I show God my love and respect?

What does the Lord your God require of you,
but to fear the Lord your God, to walk in all
his ways, and to love him, and to serve the
Lord your God with all your heart and with
all your soul.

Deuteronomy 10:12 KJV

So then, my brothers, because of God's great
mercy to us, I make this appeal to you: Offer
yourselves as a living sacrifice to God, dedicated
to his service and pleasing to him. This is the
true worship that you should offer.

Romans 12:1 TEV

He has told you, O mortal, what is good; and
what does the Lord require of you but to do
justice, and to love kindness, and to walk
humbly with your God?

Micah 6:8 NRSV

If anyone loves me, he will obey my teaching.
My Father will love him, and we will come to
him and make our home with him. *John 14:23 NIV*

Do not continue to work for the food that spoils
but for the food that keeps until everlasting life,
which the Son of Man will give you because
God the Father has placed his seal of approval
on him. They asked him, "What are the works
that God wants us to do?" Jesus answered
them, "This is the work of God that you believe
in him whom he sent." *John 6:27-29 GW*

God Remains Faithful

My faith is shaky and I have many doubts.
Does God turn away from me when
I am uncertain about him?

Even when we are too weak to have any faith
left, he remains faithful to us and will help us,
he cannot disown us who are part of himself,
and he will always carry out his promises to us.

2 Timothy 2:13 TLB

By grace are you saved through faith; and that
not of yourselves; it is the gift of God.

Ephesians 2:8 KJV

As a father has compassion on his children, so
the Lord has compassion on those who fear
him; for he knows how we are formed, he
remembers that we are dust.

Psalm 103:13-14 NIV

I am persuaded, that neither death, nor life, nor angels, nor principalities, nor powers, nor things present, nor things to come, nor height, nor depth, nor any other creature, shall be able to separate us from the love of God, which is in Christ Jesus our Lord.

Romans 8:38-39 KJV

God Forgives

*I have confessed my failures to God,
but they keep haunting me.
How can I be sure of God's forgiveness?*

I have swept away your transgressions like a cloud, and your sins like mist; return to me, for I have redeemed you.

Isaiah 44:22 NRSV

O Lord, you are so good and kind, so ready to forgive; so full of mercy for all who ask your aid.

Psalm 86:5 TLB

If we confess our sins, he is faithful and just to forgive us our sins, and to cleanse us from all unrighteousness.

1 John 1:9 KJV

Let the wicked forsake his way, and the unrighteous man his thoughts; and let him return unto the Lord, and he will have mercy upon him, and to our God, for he will abundantly pardon.

Isaiah 55:7 KJV

But when they kept on asking him, he stood up and said, "The person who is without sin among you should be the first to throw a stone at her." Then he bent down again and wrote on the ground. Those who heard Jesus were convicted by their conscience and went out one by one, beginning with the older men, until all had gone. Jesus was left alone with the woman in the middle of the place. Jesus stood up, "Woman, where are they?" He asked her, "Did no one condemn you?" She said "No one, Lord." Jesus said, "I do not condemn you either; Go, and from now on do not sin anymore."

John 8:7-11 GW

God Gives My Life Purpose

My days seem to be dragging. Does God have any meaningful plans for my life?

For surely I know the plans I have for you, says the Lord, plans for your welfare and not for harm, to give you a future with hope.

Jeremiah 29:11 NRSV

You did not choose me, but I chose you, and appointed you, that you should go and bear fruit, and that your fruit should remain: that whatever you ask the Father in my name, he may give you.

John 15:16 NKJV

You chart the path ahead of me, and tell me where to stop and rest. Every moment, you know where I am. You both precede and follow me, and place your hand of blessing on my head.

Psalm 139:3, 5 TLB

We urge you, beloved to admonish the idlers, encourage the faint hearted, help the weak, be patient with all of them. See that none of you repays evil for evil, but always seek to do good to one another and to all. Rejoice always, pray without ceasing, give thanks in all circumstances; for this is the will of God in Christ Jesus for you.

1 Thessalonians 5:14-18 NRSV

Nevertheless I am continually with you; you hold my right hand. You guide me with your counsel, and afterward you will receive me with honor.

Psalm 73:23-24 NRSV

God's Goal for My Life

Much of my life is behind me.
What kind of goals does God want me
to make for the years ahead?

One thing I do, forgetting what lies behind and straining forward to what lies ahead, I press on toward the goal for the prize of the upward call of God in Christ Jesus.

Philippians 3:13-14 RSV

Do your best to present yourself to God as one approved, a workman who does not need to be ashamed and who correctly handles the word of truth.

2 Timothy 2:15 NIV

As you have therefore received Christ Jesus the Lord, so walk in him: rooted and built up in him, and established in the faith, as you have been taught, abounding in it with thanksgiving.

Colossians 2:6-7 NKJV

We can be mirrors that brightly reflect the glory of the Lord. And as the Spirit of the Lord works within us, we become more and more like him.

2 Corinthians 3:18 TLB

He guides the humble in what is right and teaches them his way.

Psalm 25:9 NIV

You did not choose me, but I chose you, and appointed you, that you should go and bear fruit, and that your fruit should remain: that whatever you ask the Father in my name, he may give you.

John 15:16 NKJV

You chart the path ahead of me, and tell me where to stop and rest. Every moment, you know where I am. You both precede and follow me, and place your hand of blessing on my head.

Psalm 139:3, 5 TLB

I Can Serve God
*I have received so much from God.
What can I do for him?*

If you love me, keep my commandments.

John 14:15 KJV

This is how we know what love is: Jesus Christ laid down his life for us. And we ought to lay down our lives for our brothers.

1 John 3:16 NIV

I beseech you therefore, brethren, by the mercies of God, that you present your bodies a living sacrifice, holy, acceptable unto God, which is your reasonable service.

Romans 12:1 KJV

Every day I will praise you and extol your name forever and ever.

Psalm 145:2 NIV

You shall love the Lord your God with all your heart, and with all your soul, and with all your mind. This is the first and great commandment.

Matthew 22:37-38 KJV

Whatever you do, work at it with all your heart, as working for the Lord, not for men, since you know that you will receive an inheritance from the Lord as a reward. It is the Lord Christ you are serving.

Colossians 3:23-24 NIV

God Is Always with Me
When I don't feel God's presence, does that mean he is not with me?

He has said, "I will never leave you, nor forsake you."

Hebrews 13:5 KJV

I am with you always, even unto the end of the world.

Matthew 28:20 KJV

Then shall you call, and the Lord shall answer;
you shall cry, and he shall say, Here I am.

Isaiah 58:9 KJV

How precious it is, Lord, to realize that you are
thinking about me constantly! I can't even
count how many times a day your thoughts
turn towards me. And when I waken in the
morning, you are still thinking of me!

Psalm 139:17-18 TLB

Who shall separate us from the love of Christ?
Shall tribulation, or distress, or persecution, or
famine, or nakedness, or peril, or sword? For I
am persuaded, that neither death, nor life, nor
angels, nor principalities, nor powers, nor things
present, nor things to come, nor height, nor
depth, nor any other creature, shall be able to
separate us from the love of God, which is in
Christ Jesus our Lord.

Romans 8:35, 38-39 KJV

God Helps Me Grow
I want my faith to grow!
How can I learn to trust God?

The Lord will make you go through hard times,
but he himself will be there to teach you, and
you will not have to search for him anymore. If
you wander off the road to the right or the left,
you will hear his voice behind you saying,
"Here is the road. Follow it."

Isaiah 30:20-21 TEV

Seek the Lord and his strength, seek his face
constantly.

1 Chronicles 16:11 KJV

The Comforter, which is the Holy Spirit, whom
the Father will send in my name, he shall teach
you all things, and bring all things to your
remembrance, whatsoever I have said unto you.

John 14:26 KJV

When all kinds of trials and temptations crowd
into your lives, my brothers, don't resent them
as intruders, but welcome them as friends!
Realize that they come to test your faith and to
produce in you the quality of endurance.

James 1:2-3 Phillips

Ah Lord God! Behold, you have made the
heaven and the earth by your great power and
stretched out arm, and there is nothing too hard
for you.... Behold, I am the Lord, the God of all
flesh: is there any thing too hard for me?

Jeremiah 32:17,27 KJV

Yours, O Lord, is the greatness and the power
and the glory and the majesty and the splendor,
for everything in heaven and earth is yours.
Yours, O Lord, is the kingdom; you are exalted
as head over all. Wealth and honor come from
you; you are the ruler of all things. In your
hands are strength and power to exalt and give
strength to all.

1 Chronicles 29:11-12 NIV

Every good and perfect gift is from above, coming down from the Father of the heavenly lights, who does not change like shifting shadows.

James 1:17 NIV

Before you created the hills or brought the world into being, you were eternally God, and will be God forever.

Psalm 90:2 TEV

God Speaks to Me
*I haven't read the Bible much
during my life. I have more time now.
Will God really speak to me?*

All those words which were written long ago are meant to teach us today; so that we may be encouraged to endure and to go on hoping in our own time.

Romans 15:4 Phillips

All Scripture is given by inspiration of God, and is profitable for doctrine, for reproof, for correction, for instruction in righteousness: That the man of God may be perfect, thoroughly furnished unto all good works.

2 Timothy 3:16-17 KJV

Your word is a lamp unto my feet, and a light unto my path. The entrance of your words gives light; it gives understanding unto the simple.

Psalm 119:105, 130 KJV

Your words are what sustain me; they are food to my hungry soul. They bring joy to my sorrowing heart and delight me.

Jeremiah 15:16 TLB

If you continue in my word, then you are my disciples indeed; and you shall know the truth, and the truth shall make you free.

John 8:31-32 KJV

The word of God is living and active. Sharper than any double-edged sword, it penetrates even to dividing soul and spirit, joints and marrow; it judges the thoughts and attitudes of the heart.

Hebrews 4:12 NIV

God Makes Me Feel Secure

God Guides Me
God Protects Me
God Gives Me Peace
God Gives Me Joy
God Gives Me Hope
I Am Thankful to God
God Gives Me Comfort
God Always Provides

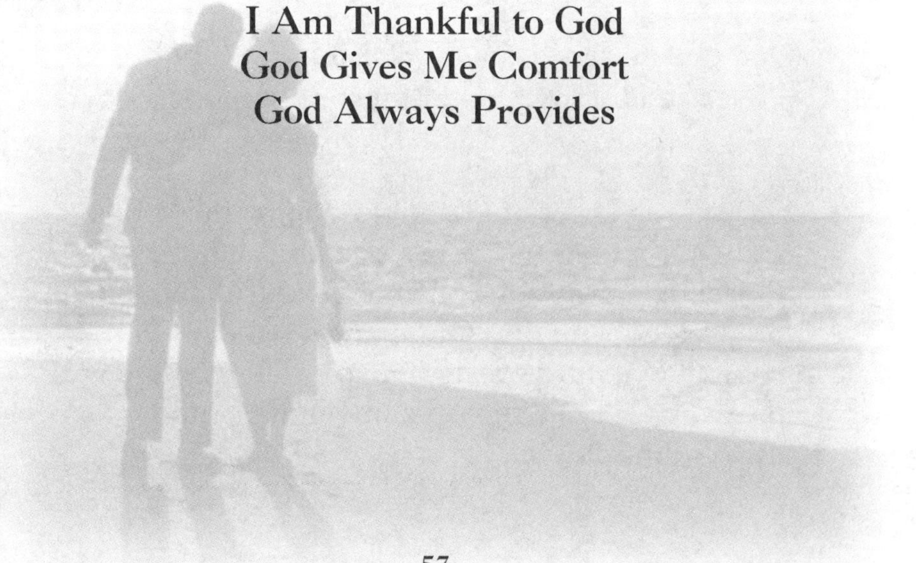

God Guides Me

*As my life changes, I sometimes feel
confused or unstable. Can God provide
the guidance and safety I need?*

The Lord, he it is that does go before you; he
will be with you, he will not fail you, neither
forsake you: fear not, neither be dismayed.

Deuteronomy 31:8 KJV

God has not given us the spirit of fear; but of
power, and of love, and of a sound mind.

2 Timothy 1:7 KJV

He will never let me stumble, slip or fall. For he
is always watching, never sleeping. Jehovah
himself is caring for you! He is your defender.
He protects you day and night. He keeps you
from all evil, and preserves your life. He keeps
his eye upon you as you come and go, and
always guards you.

Psalm 121:3-8 TLB

My grace is sufficient for you; for my strength is made perfect in weakness.

2 Corinthians 12:9 KJV

Know therefore that the Lord your God, he is God, the faithful God, who keeps his covenant and his loving kindness to a thousand generations with those who love him and keep his commandments.

Deuteronomy 7:9 NASB

Let him have all your worries and cares, for he is always thinking about you and watching everything that concerns you.

1 Peter 5:7 TLB

No evil shall befall you, no scounge come near your tent. For he will command his angels concerning you to guard you in all your ways.

Psalm 91:10-11 NRSV

I hereby command you: Be strong and courageous; do not be frightened or dismayed, for the Lord your God is with you wherever you go.

Joshua 1:9 NRSV

Trust in the Lord with all your heart, and do not rely on your own insight. In all your ways acknowledge him, and he will make straight your paths.

Proverbs 3:5-6 NRSV

God Protects Me

I feel anxious because others are making decisions for me with which I disagree.

The Lord shall preserve you from all evil: he shall preserve your soul. The Lord shall preserve your going out and coming in from this time forth, and even for evermore.

Psalm 121:7-8 KJV

The Lord is my strength and my shield; my heart trusts in him, and I am helped. My heart leaps for joy and I will give thanks to him in song.

Psalm 28:7 NIV

You will keep him in perfect peace, whose mind is stayed on you: because he trusts in you.

Isaiah 26:3 KJV

If God be for us, who can be against us?

Romans 8:31 KJV

Wait on the Lord: be of good courage, and he shall strengthen your heart: wait, I say, on the Lord.

Psalm 27:14 KJV

God Gives Me Peace

How can I find peace when
I feel anxious about the unknown,
uncertain things in life?

Have no anxiety about anything, but in everything by prayer and supplication with thanksgiving let your requests be made known to God.
And the peace of God, which passes all understanding, will keep your hearts and your minds
in Christ Jesus.

Philippians 4:6-7 RSV

Peace I leave with you, my peace I give unto you;
not as the world gives, give I unto you. Let not
your heart be troubled, neither let it be afraid.

John 14:27 KJV

These things I have spoken unto you, that in me you might have peace. In the world you shall have tribulation: but be of good cheer. I have overcome the world.

John 16:33 KJV

The Lord loves the just and will not forsake his faithful ones. They will be protected forever.

Psalm 37:28 NIV

God Gives Me Joy
*How can I be full of joy when
I am feeling down?*

Behold, I bring you good tidings of great joy, which shall be to all people. For unto you is born this day in the city of David a Savior, which is Christ the Lord.

Luke 2:10-11 KJV

I will rejoice in the Lord, I will joy in the God of my salvation.

Habakkuk 3:18 KJV

You show me the path of life; in your presence there is fullness of you, in your right hand are pleasures for evermore.

Psalm 16:11 RSV

I will greatly rejoice in the Lord, my soul shall be joyful in my God; for he has clothed me with the garments of salvation, he has covered me with the robe of righteousness, as a bridegroom decks himself with ornaments, and as a bride adorns herself with her jewels.

Isaiah 61:10 KJV

Delight yourselves in the Lord, yes, find your joy in him all times...Never forget the nearness of your Lord.

Philippians 4:4-5 Phillips

Just as you received Christ Jesus the Lord, so
go on living in him—in simple faith. Yes, be
rooted in him and founded upon him, continually strengthened by the faith as you were taught
it and your lives will overflow with joy and
thankfulness.

Colossians 2:6-7 Phillpis

God Gives Me Hope
How can I overcome depression?

Base your happiness on your hope in Christ.
When trials come endure them patiently; stead-
fastly maintain the habit of prayer.

Romans 12:12 Phillips

The Lord is close to the brokenhearted and
saves those who are crushed in spirit.

Psalm 34:18 NIV

O my soul, why be so gloomy and discouraged?
Trust in God! I shall again praise him for his
wondrous help; he will make me smile again,
for he is my God!

Psalm 43:5 TLB

Our light affliction, which is but for a moment,
works for us a far more exceeding and eternal
weight of glory; while we look not at the things
which are seen, but at the things which are not
seen: for the things which are seen are temporal;
but the things which are not seen are eternal.

Corinthians 4:17-18 KJV

Just as you received Christ Jesus the Lord, so
go on living in him—in simple faith. Yes, be
rooted in him and founded upon him, continually strengthened by the faith as you were taught
it and your lives will overflow with joy and
thankfulness.

Colossians 2:6-7 Phillips

I Am Thankful to God

*I seem to be spending more and
more time alone. How can I turn this
into something good rather than
letting it get me down?*

Singing and making melody in your heart to the
Lord; giving thanks always for all things unto
God and the Father in the name of our Lord
Jesus Christ.

Ephesians 5:19b-20 KJV

Base your happiness on your hope in Christ.
When trials come endure them patiently; stead-
fastly maintain the habit of prayer.

Romans 12:12 Phillips

Let each of you look not only to his own interests, but also to the interests of others.

Philippians 2:4 RSV

I will call to mind the deed of the Lord; I will remember your wonders of old. I will meditate on all your work, and muse on your mighty deeds.

Psalm 77:11-12 NRSV

God Gives Me Comfort
If God has promised to be with me, why do I feel lonely?

Seek the Lord while he may be found, call upon him while he is near: let the wicked forsake his way, and the unrighteous man his thoughts: let him return to the Lord, and he will have mercy on him; and to our God, for he will abundantly pardon.

Isaiah 55:6-7 NKJV

The Lord is just in all his ways and kind in all his doings. The Lord is near to all who call upon him, to all who call upon him in truth.

Psalm 145:17-18 RSV

Who shall separate us from the love of Christ? Shall tribulation, or distress, or persecution, or famine, or nakedness, or peril, or sword? No, in all these things we are more than conquerors through him that loved us.

Romans 8:35, 37 KJV

God Always Provides

Sometimes I worry about finances.
Will God provide for my needs?

The Lord himself is my inheritance, my prize. He is my food and drink, my highest joy! He guards all that is mine. He sees that I am given pleasant brooks and meadows as my share! What a wonderful inheritance.

Psalm 16:5-6 TLB

He who did not grudge his own Son but gave him up for us all—can we not trust such a God to give us, with him, everything else that we can need?

Romans 8:32 Phillips

I will always guide you and satisfy you with good things. I will keep you strong and well. You will be like a garden that has plenty of water, like a spring of water that never goes dry.

Isaiah 58:11 TEV

You open your hand and satisfy the desire of every living thing. The Lord is righteous in all his ways and loving toward all he has made. The Lord is near to all who call on him in truth. He fulfills the desires of those who fear him; he hears their cry and saves them.

Psalm 145:16-19 NIV

Better is a little that the righteous person has than the abundance of many wicked. For the arms of the wicked shall be broken, but the Lord upholds the righteous.

Psalm 37:16-17 NRSV

The young lions suffer want and hunger, but those who seek the Lord lack no good thing.

Psalm 34:10 NRSV

Trust in the Lord, and do good; so you will live in the land, and enjoy security. Take delight in the Lord, and he will give you the desires of your heart.

Psalm 37:3-4 NRSV

When I Am Hurting

God Is Always There For Me
God Understands Me
God Gives Me Strength
God Is My Security
God Answers My Prayers
God Gives Me Rest
God Strengthens My Faith
God Will Help Me
God Won't Forsake Me
God Knows My Heart
I Can Still Share God
I Can Still Serve God
With God My Future is Bright
God Can Make Me Pleasant

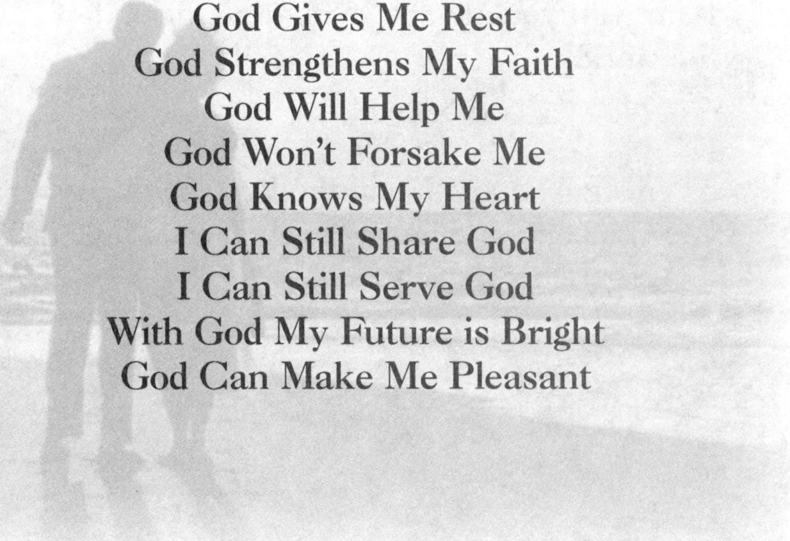

God Is Always There for Me

I feel alone with my physical pain; no one else can feel it with me. How can I know God is with me when I am hurting?

He has said, "I will never leave you, nor forsake you."

Hebrews 13:5 KJV

I am with you always, even unto the end of the world.

Matthew 28:20 KJV

Then shall you call, and the Lord shall answer; you shall cry, and he shall say, Here I am.

Isaiah 58:9 KJV

How precious it is, Lord, to realize that you are thinking about me constantly! I can't even count how many times a day your thoughts turn toward me. And when I waken in the morning, you are still thinking of me!

Psalm 139:17-18 TLB

I will be your God through all your lifetime, yes, even when your hair is white with age. I made you and I will care for you. I will carry you along and be your savior.

Isaiah 46:4 TLB

You hear, O Lord, the desire of the afflicted; you encourage them, and you listen to their cry, defending the fatherless and the oppressed, in order that man, who is of the earth, may terrify no more.

Psalm 10:17-18 NIV

My flesh and my heart may fail, but God is the strength of my heart and my portion forever.

Psalm 73:26 NRSV

Cast your burden on the Lord, and he will sustain you; he will never permit the righteous to be moved.

Psalm 55:22 NRSV

God Understands Me
If I become inarticulate or confused, will I still be able to communicate with God?

The Spirit helps us in our weakness. We do not know what we ought to pray, but the Spirit himself intercedes for us with groans that words cannot express.

Romans 8:26 NIV

He withdraws not his eyes from the righteous.

Job 36:7a KJV

I am continually with you: you have held me by my right hand. You shall guide me with your counsel, and afterward receive me to glory.

Psalm 73:23-24 KJV

O Lord, you have searched and you know me. You know when I sit and when I rise; you perceive my thoughts from afar. You discern my going out and my lying down; you are familiar with all my ways. Before a word is on my tongue you know it completely, O Lord.

Psalm 139:1-4 NIV

God Gives Me Strength

*Will God give me the strength to endure
sickness and pain?*

The Lord is my light and my salvation; whom
shall I fear? The Lord is the strength of my life;
of whom shall I be afraid?

Psalm 27:1 KJV

Cast your cares on the Lord and he will sustain
you; he will never let the righteous fall.

Psalm 55:22 NIV

My God shall supply all your need according to
his riches in glory by Christ Jesus.

Philippians 4:19 KJV

He gives power to the faint and to them that have no might he increases strength; they shall mount up with wings as eagles; they shall run, and not be weary; and they shall walk, and not faint.

Isaiah 40:29-31 KJV

Trust in the Lord God always, for the Lord Jehovah is your everlasting strength.

Isaiah 26:4 TLB

Why are you cast down, O my soul, and why are you disquieted within me? Hope in God; for I shall again praise him, my help and my God.

Psalm 42:11 NRSV

In the day of my trouble I call on you, for you will answer me.

Psalm 86:7 NRSV

Are any among you sick? They should call for
the elders of the church and have them pray
over them, anointing them with oil in the name
of the Lord. The prayer of faith will save the
sick, and the Lord will raise them up: and anyone who has committed sins will be forgiven.

James 5:14-15 NRSV

Heal me, O Lord, and I shall be healed; save
me, and I shall be saved; for you are my praise.

Jeremiah 17:14 NRSV

Then they cried to the Lord in their trouble,
and he saved them from their distress; he sent
out his word and healed them, and delivered
them from destruction.

Psalm 107:19-20 NRSV

God Is My Security

Sometimes when I'm afraid or anxious, I feel physically ill. How can I feel secure and unafraid?

The Lord is my light and my salvation; whom shall I fear? The Lord is the strength of my life; of whom shall I be afraid?

Psalm 27:1 KJV

Bless the Lord, O my soul, and forget not all his benefits, who forgives all your iniquity, who heals all your diseases, who redeems your life from the pit, who crowns you with steadfast love and mercy, who satisfies you with good as long as you live so that your youth is renewed like the eagle's.

Psalm 103:2-5 RSV

Fear not, for I have redeemed you, I have
called you by your name; you are mine.

Isaiah 43:1 KJV

When you pass through the waters, I will be
with you; and through the rivers, they shall not
overflow you; when you walk through the fire,
you shall not be burned; neither shall the flame
kindle upon you. For I am the Lord your God,
the Holy One of Israel, your Savior.

Isaiah 43:2-3 KJV

Just as you trusted Christ to save you, trust
him, too, for each day's problems; live in vital
union with him.

Colossians 2:6 TLB

Let him have all your worries and cares, for he
is always thinking about you and watching
everything that concerns you.

1 Peter 5:7 TLB

If you sit down, you will not be afraid; when you lie down, your sleep will be sweet. Do not be afraid of sudden panic, or of the storm that strikes the wicked; for the Lord will be your confidence and will keep your foot from being caught.

Proverbs 3:24-26 NRSV

God Answers My Prayers

When physical limitations prevent me from leaving the house, I stay at home and pray. Will my prayers accomplish anything?

Whatsoever we ask, we receive of him, because we keep his commandments, and do those things that are pleasing in his sight. And this is his commandment, that we should believe on the name of his Son Jesus Christ, and love one another, as he gave us commandment.

1 John 3:22-23 KJV

Have no anxiety about anything, but in everything, by prayer and supplication with thanksgiving let your requests be made known to God. And the peace of God, which passes all understanding, will keep your hearts and minds in Christ Jesus.

Philippians 4:6-7 RSV

This is the confidence which we have in him, that if we ask anything according to his will he hears us.

1 John 5:14 RSV

I will pray morning, noon, and night, pleading aloud with God; and he will hear and answer.

Psalm 55:17 TLB

Even before they finish praying to me, I will answer their prayers.

Isaiah 65:24 TEV

And all things, whatever you shall ask in prayer, believing, you shall receive.

Matthew 21:22 KJV

If you abide in me, and my words abide in you, you shall ask what you will, and it shall be done unto you.

John 15:7 KJV

So confess your sins to one another, and pray for one another to be healed. The earnest prayer of a righteous person accomplishes much.

James 5:16 GW

God Gives Me Rest

Can the Lord help me rest at night when I am unable to sleep?

I lie down and sleep; I wake again, for the Lord sustains me.

Psalm 3:5 RSV

He gives his beloved sleep.

Psalm 127:2b KJV

Come to me, all you who are weary and burdened, and I will give you rest. Take my yoke upon you and learn from me, for I am gentle and humble in heart, and you will find rest for your souls. For my yoke is easy and my burden is light.

Matthew 11:28-30 NIV

He who dwells in the shelter of the Most High will rest in the shadow of the Almighty.

Psalm 91:1 NIV

If you sit down, you will not be afraid; When you lie down, your sleep will be sweet.

Proverbs 3:24 NRSV

God Strengthens My Faith

*On days when I feel physically weak,
how can I help my faith grow strong?*

We do not lose heart. Though outwardly we are
wasting away, yet inwardly we are being
renewed day by day. For our light and momen-
tary troubles are achieving for us an eternal
glory that far outweighs them all. So we fix our
eyes not on what is seen, but on what is unseen.
For what is seen is temporary, but what is
unseen is eternal.

2 Corinthians 4:16-18 NIV

As you have therefore received Christ Jesus the
Lord, so walk in him: rooted and built up in
him, and established in the faith, as you have
been taught, abounding in it with thanksgiving.

Colossians 2:6-7 NKJV

Let us therefore come boldly unto the throne of grace, that we may obtain mercy, and find grace to help in time of need.

Hebrews 4:16 KJV

Even when we are too weak to have any faith left, he remains faithful to us and will help us, for he cannot disown us who are part of himself, and he will always carry out his promises to us.

2 Timothy 2:13 TLB

God Will Help Me

Sometimes I'm afraid that my physical limitations will be embarrassing to my loved ones.

Fear not, for you shall not be ashamed: neither be confounded, for you shall not be put to shame...With everlasting kindness will I have mercy on you, says the Lord your Redeemer.

Isaiah 54:4a, 8b KJV

I lift up my eyes to the hills—from where will my help come? My help comes from the Lord, who made heaven and earth. He will not let your foot be moved; he who keeps you will not slumber. The Lord is your keeper; the Lord is your shade at your right hand.

Psalm 121:1-3, 5 NRSV

I the Lord your God will hold your right hand, saying unto you: Fear not; I will help you.

Isaiah 41:13 KJV

I will bring the blind by a way that they knew not; I will lead them in paths that they have not known: I will make darkness light before them, and crooked things straight. These things will I do unto them, and not forsake them.

Isaiah 42:16 KJV

God Won't Forsake Me

*If someday I can no longer control
my actions and speech, might I bring
dishonor to the Lord?*

Even to your old age and gray hairs I am he, I
am he who will sustain you. I have made you
and I will carry you; I will sustain you and I
will rescue you.

Isaiah 46:4 NIV

The very God of peace sanctify you wholly: and
I pray God your whole spirit and soul and body
be preserved blameless unto the coming of our
Lord Jesus Christ. Faithful is he that calls you,
who also will do it.

1 Thessalonians 5:23-24 KJV

The Lord, he is the one who goes before you.
He will be with you, he will not leave you nor
forsake you; do not fear nor be dismayed.

Deuteronomy 31:8 NKJV

Now unto him that is able to keep you from falling, and to present you faultless before the presence of his glory with exceeding joy, to the only wise God our Savior, be glory and majesty, dominion and power, both now and forever. Amen.

Jude 1:24-25 KJV

They will be like a well-watered garden, and they will sorrow no more... I will turn their mourning into gladness; I will give them comfort and joy instead of sorrow.

Jeremiah 31:12-13 NIV

God Knows My Heart

Sometimes I feel self-conscious because age has changed my appearance. How does God see me?

You shall also be a crown of glory in the hand of the Lord, and a royal diadem in the hand of your God.

Isaiah 62:3 NKJV

The Lord sees not as man sees; for man looks on the outward appearance, but the Lord looks on the heart.

1 Samuel 16:7 KJV

O worship the Lord in the beauty of holiness.

Psalm 96:9 KJV

White hair is a crown of glory and is seen most among the godly.

Proverbs 16:31 TLB

Even to your old age and gray hairs, I am he, I am he who will sustain you.

Isaiah 46:4 NIV

I Can Still Share God

As I become more limited in my ability to get out or to travel, how can I keep sharing my faith and my Christian experience with others?

The righteous will flourish like a palm tree, they will grow like a cedar of Lebanon; planted in the house of the Lord, they will flourish in the courts of our God. They will still bear fruit in old age, they will stay fresh and green, proclaiming "The Lord is upright; he is my Rock, and there is no wickedness in him."

Psalm 92:12-15 NIV

Sanctify the Lord God in your hearts: and be ready always to give an answer to every man that asks you a reason of the hope that is in you with meekness and fear.

1 Peter 3:15 KJV

You may live a life worthy of the Lord and may please him in every way: bearing fruit in every good work, growing in the knowledge of God, being strengthened with all power according to his glorious might so that you may have great endurance and patience, and joyfully giving thanks to the Father, who has qualified you to share in the inheritance of the saints in the kingdom of light.

Colossians 1:10-12 NIV

For God did not give us a spirit of timidity, but a spirit of power, of love, and of self-discipline.

2 Timothy 1:7 NIV

I Can Still Serve God

*Because of physical limitations, I am
unable to serve the Lord in the way I used to.
How can I serve him now?*

Warn them that are unruly, comfort the feeble-
minded, support the weak, be patient toward all
men. See that none render evil for evil unto any
man; but ever follow that which is good, both
among yourselves, and to all men. Rejoice evermore. Pray without ceasing. In every thing give
thanks: for this is the will of God in Christ Jesus
concerning you.

1 Thessalonians 5:14-18 KJV

Then the King will say to those on his right
hand, Come, you blessed of my Father, inherit
the kingdom prepared for you from the founda-
tion of the world: for I was hungry, and you
gave me food: I was thirsty, and you gave me
drink: I was a stranger, and you took me in:

I was naked, and you clothed me: I was sick, and you visited me: I was in prison, and you came to me. Inasmuch as you did it unto one of the least of these my brethren, you did it to me.

Matthew 25:34-36 NKJV

Giving all diligence, add to your faith virtue; and to virtue knowledge; and to knowledge temperance; and to temperance patience; and to patience godliness; and to godliness brotherly kindness; and to brotherly kindness charity. For if these things be in you, and abound, they make you that you shall neither be barren nor unfruitful in the knowledge of our Lord Jesus Christ.

2 Peter 1:5-8 KJV

O worship the Lord in the beauty of holiness.

Psalm 96:9 KJV

With God My Future Is Bright

*Now that I'm older, I still want to get
excited about life and be involved,
but what do I have to look forward to?*

You show me the path of life; in your presence
there is fullness of joy, in your right hand are
pleasures forevermore.

Psalm 16:11 RSV

You have everything when you have Christ,
and you are filled with God through your union
with Christ.

Colossians 2:10 TLB

Delight yourselves in the Lord, yes, find your
joy in him at all times...Never forget the nearness of your Lord.

Philippians 4:4-5 Phillips

He guides the humble in what is right and teaches them his way. Who, then, is the man that fears the Lord? He will instruct him in the way chosen for him.

Psalm 25:9, 12 NIV

I have come that they might have life, and that they might have it more abundantly.

John 10:10b KJV

I know the plans I have for you, says the Lord, plans for welfare and not for evil, to give you a future and a hope.

Jeremiah 29:11 RSV

The Spirit himself bears witness with our spirit that we are children of God, and if children, heirs also, heirs of God and fellow heirs with Christ, if indeed we suffer with him in order that we may also be glorified with him.

Romans 8:16-17 NASB

God Can Make Me Pleasant

I want to be more pleasant, but some things tend to irritate me more than they used to. What can I do about my temperament?

Be kind one to another, tenderhearted, forgiving one another, even as God for Christ's sake has forgiven you.

Ephesians 4:32 KJV

Bless the Lord, O my soul: and all that is within me, bless his holy name. Bless the Lord, O my soul, and forget not all his benefits.

Psalm 103:1-2 KJV

As you know him better, he will give you, through his great power, everything you need for living a truly good life: he even shares his own glory and his own goodness with us!

2 Peter 1:3 TLB

Finally, all of you, live in harmony, be sympathetic, love your fellow Christians, be tenderhearted and humble, do not pay back evil for evil, insult for insult, but speak a blessing instead. That is what you were called to do—so that you might inherit a blessing. If a person wants to love life and enjoy happy days, let him stop speaking evil or saying anything deceitful, let him turn away from wrong and do good; let him be eager for peace and pursue it. For the Lord watches the righteous and hears their prayer, but the Lord is against those who do wrong.

1 Peter 3:8-12 GW

My Family

My Family Is Important to God
I Can Influence My Family Now
I Can Influence My Family Forever
God Will Always Care For My Family
God Can Guide Me Through
Family Problems
God Will Rescue Prodigal Children
God Can Overcome My Mistakes
God Can Keep Families Together
God Helps Me When My Spouse Changes
God Gives Me Independence
God Makes Me Thankful
God Consoles My Loneliness
God Still Needs Me
God Takes Away My Bitterness
God Rebuilds My Burned Bridges

My Family Is Important to God

*My family has been important to
me all my life. Does God value my
children and grandchildren?*

Children's children are the crown of old men;
and the glory of children are their fathers.

Proverbs 17:6 KJV

Lo, children are a heritage of the Lord; and the
fruit of the womb is his reward. As arrows are
in the hand of a mighty man; so are children of
the youth. Happy is the man that has his quiver
full of them.

Psalm 127:3-5a KJV

May the Lord bless you from Zion all the days
of your life; may you see the prosperity of
Jerusalem, and may you live to see your children's children. Peace be upon Israel.

Psalm 128:5-6 NIV

May the Lord make you increase, both you and
your children. May you be blessed by the Lord,
the Maker of Heaven and earth.

Psalm 115:14 NIV

The Son of man came to save the lost. "What
do you think? If a man has a hundred sheep
and one of them strays away, will he not leave
the ninety-nine in the hills and go and look for
the straying sheep? And if he finds it, I tell you
the truth, he is happier about it than about the
ninety-nine that have not strayed away. In the
same way your Father in heaven does not want
one of these little ones to be lost."

Matthew 18:11-14 GW

I Can Influence My Family Now
How can my actions build a godly heritage for my children and their children?

The just man walks in his integrity: his children are blessed after him.

Proverbs 20:7 KJV

The counsel of the Lord stands forever, the thoughts of his heart to all generations.

Psalm 33:11 KJV

Give yourself to the Lord; trust in him, and he will help you; he will make your righteousness shine like the noonday sun.

Psalm 37:5-6 TEV

He who fears the Lord has a secure fortress, and for his children it will be a refuge.

Proverbs 14:26 NIV

And all your children shall be taught of the Lord; and great shall be the peace of your children.

Isaiah 54:13 KJV

Train up a child in the way he should go: And when he is old, he will not depart from it.

Proverbs 22:6 KJV

I Can Influence My Family Forever
I am concerned about my children and my grandchildren. What can I do now to keep them growing in the Lord even after I'm not with them anymore?

Only be careful, and watch yourselves closely so that you do not forget the things your eyes have seen or let them slip from your heart as long as you live. Teach them to your children and to the children after them.

Deuteronomy 4:9 NIV

And these words, which I command you this day, shall be in your heart: And you shall teach them diligently unto your children, and shall talk of them when you sit in your house, and when you walk by the way, and when you lie down, and when you rise up.

Deuteronomy 6:6-7 KJV

Gather the people together, men, and women, and children, and the stranger that is within the gates, that they may hear, and they may learn, and fear the Lord your God, and observe to do all the words of the law: And that their children, which have not known anything, may hear, and learn to fear the Lord your God.

Deuteronomy 31:12-13 KJV

But the mercy of the Lord is from everlasting to everlasting upon them that fear him, and his righteousness unto children's children, to such as keep his covenant, and to those that remember his commandments to do them.

Psalm 103:17 KJV

Give ear, O my people, to my teaching: incline your ears to the words of my mouth... Things that we have heard and known, that our ancestors have told us. We will not hide them from their children, we will tell to the coming generation the glorious deeds of the Lord and his might, and the wonders that he has done.

Psalm 78:1, 3-4 NRSV

Train up a child in the way he should go: and when he is old, he will not depart from it.

Proverbs 22:6 KJV

For he established a testimony in Jacob, and appointed a law in Israel, which he commanded our fathers, that they should make them known to their children: That the generation to come might know them... That they might set their hope in God, and not forget the works of God, but keep his commandments.

Psalm 78:5-6a,7 KJV

God Will Always Care For My Family

Sometimes I feel sad that I won't be able to look after my children and grandchildren for many more years. How can I feel assured that God will take care of them?

I have been young, and now I am old; yet I have not seen the righteous forsaken or his children begging bread.

Psalm 37:25 RSV

The young lions do lack, and suffer hunger:
but they that seek the Lord shall not want any
good thing.

Psalm 34:10 KJV

He who did not grudge his own Son but gave
him up for us all—can we not trust such a God
to give us, with him, everything else that we
can need?

Romans 8:32 Phillips

Know therefore that the Lord your God is God;
he is the faithful God, keeping his covenant of
love to a thousand generations of those who
love him and keep his commands.

Deuteronomy 7:9 NIV

The righteous man leads a blameless life;
blessed are his children after him.

Proverbs 20:7 NIV

God Can Guide Me Through Family Problems

At times I'm concerned about the tensions in some of my family relationships. How does God want me to respond?

If you are offering your gift at the altar and there remember that your brother has something against you, leave your gift there in front of the altar. First go and be reconciled to your brother; then come and offer your gift.

Matthew 5:23-24 NIV

Be kind and compassionate to one another, forgiving each other, just as in Christ God forgave you.

Ephesians 4:32 NIV

Bear with each other and forgive whatever grievances you may have against one another. Forgive as the Lord forgave you. *Colossians 3:13 NIV*

....then make my joy complete being like-minded, having the same love, being one in spirit and purpose... Your attitude should be the same as that of Christ Jesus. *Philippians 2:2,5 NIV*

Try to stay out of all quarrels and seek to live a clean and holy life, for one who is not holy will not see the Lord. *Hebrews 12:14 TLB*

He who covers over an offense promotes love, but whoever repeats the matter separates close friends. *Proverbs 17:9 NIV*

God Will Rescue Prodigal Children

Although I have brought up my children to live godly lives, some of them are not living for God. How can I keep hoping for them?

He is patient with you, not wanting anyone to perish, but everyone to come to repentance.

2 Peter 3:9 NIV

Have no anxiety about anything, but in everything by prayer and supplication with thanksgiving let your requests be made known to God. And the peace of God, which passes all understanding, will keep your hearts and your minds in Christ Jesus.

Philippians 4:6-7 RSV

Train children in the right way, and when old, they will not stray.

Proverbs 22:6 NRSV

It is of the Lord's mercies that we are not con-
sumed, because his compassions fail not. They
are new every morning: great is your faithfulness. It is good that a man should both hope and
quietly wait for the salvation of the Lord.

Lamentations 3:22-23, 26 KJV

God Can Overcome My Mistakes

*Some of the choices I made as a parent
were damaging to my children.
I know God has forgiven me, but can
God turn my mistakes into something good for
my children and their children?*

Glory be to God who by his mighty power at
work within us is able to do far more than we
would ever dare to ask or even dream of—infi-
nitely beyond our highest prayers, desires,
thoughts, or hopes.

Ephesians 3:20 TLB

With men this is impossible; but with God all things are possible.

Matthew 19:26b KJV

If you turn again unto the Lord, your brethren and your children shall find compassion before them that lead them captive, so that they shall come again into this land: for the Lord your God is gracious and merciful, and will not turn away his face from you, if you return unto him.

2 Chronicles 30:9 KJV

The Lord is near unto all them that call upon him, to all that call upon him in truth. He will fulfill the desire of them that fear him: he also will hear their cry, and will save them.

Psalm 145:18-19 KJV

But from everlasting to everlasting the Lord's love is with those who fear him, and his righteousness with their children's children—with those who keep his covenant and remember to obey his precepts.

Psalm 103:17-18 NIV

God Can Keep Families Together

Although my children have families of their own, I want our extended family to grow together. How can we be unified?

Instead, speaking the truth in love, we will in all things grow up into him who is the Head, that is, Christ.

Ephesians 4:15 NIV

And let us consider how to stimulate one another to love and good deeds, not forsaking our own assembling together, as is the habit of some but encouraging one another; and all the more, as you see the day drawing near.

Hebrews 10:24-25 NASB

Speak to one another with psalms, hymns and spiritual songs. Sing and make music in your heart to the Lord, always giving thanks to God the Father for everything in the name of our Lord Jesus Christ.

Ephesians 5:19-20 NIV

You should be like one big happy family, full of sympathy toward each other, loving one another with tender hearts and humble minds.

1 Peter 3:8 TLB

Share each other's troubles and problems, and so obey our Lord's command.

Galatians 6:2 TLB

God Helps Me When My Spouse Changes
Aging has altered the personality of my loved one. How can I accept this changed relationship with someone I love?

Trust in the Lord with all your heart; and lean not unto your own understanding.

Proverbs 3:5 KJV

We know that all things work together for good to them that love God, to them who are the called according to his purpose.

Romans 8:28 KJV

A friend loves at all times, and a brother is born for adversity.

Proverbs 17:17 KJV

This is how we know what love is: Jesus Christ laid down his life for us. And we ought to lay down our lives for our brothers.

1 John 3:16 NIV

Cast your burden on the Lord, and he will sustain you; he will never permit the righteous to be removed.

Psalm 55:22 NRSV

Now then, with all these witnesses around us like a cloud, let us also rid ourselves of every burden and the sin into which we easily fall and with patient endurance run the race that is laid out before us, looking to Jesus, who gives us our faith from start to finish.

Hebrews 12:1-2 GW

God Gives Me Independence

It is hard for me not to worry about being a financial burden to my family. How does God want me to handle dependency?

Cast all your anxieties on him, for he cares about you.

1 Peter 5:7 RSV

The Lord your God has blessed you in all the works of your hand: he knows your walking through this great wilderness... the Lord your God has been with you; you have lacked nothing.

Deuteronomy 2:7 KJV

God will supply every need of yours according to his riches in glory in Christ Jesus.

Philippians 4:19 RSV

I have been young, and now I am old; yet I have not seen the righteous forsaken or his children begging bread.

Psalm 37:25 RSV

God Makes Me Thankful

Sometimes I feel resentful when I see others enjoying comfort and wealth. Can God help me to be glad for them and thankful for what I have?

Be still before the Lord, and wait patiently for him; fret not yourself over him who prospers in his way... Refrain from anger, and forsake wrath! Fret not yourself; it tends only to evil.

Psalm 37:7-8 RSV

Bless the Lord, O my soul, and forget not all his iniquities; who heals all your diseases; who redeems your life from destruction; who crowns you with lovingkindness and tender mercies; who satisfies your mouth with good things; so that your youth is renewed like the eagle's.

Psalm 103:2-5 KJV

Let all bitterness, and wrath, and anger, and clamor, and evil speaking, be put away from you, with all malice: And be kind one to another, tenderhearted, forgiving one another, even as God for Christ's sake has forgiven you.

Ephesians 4:31-32 KJV

O my soul, don't be discouraged. Don't be upset. Expect God to act! For I know that I shall again have plenty of reason to praise him for all that he will do. He is my help! He is my God!

Psalm 42:11 TLB

Trust in him at all times; you people, pour out your heart before him: God is a refuge for us.

Psalm 62:8 KJV

Better is a little that the righteous person has than the abundance of many wicked. For the arms of the wicked shall be broken, but the Lord upholds the righteous.

Psalm 37:16-17 NRSV

God Consoles My Loneliness

As old friends and loved ones pass away or move away from me, I am often sad. How can I feel encouraged by God?

I, even I, am he that comforts you.

Isaiah 51:12 KJV

He heals the broken in heart, and binds up their wounds.

Psalm 147:3 KJV

Yes, though I walk through the valley of the shadow of death, I will fear no evil: for you are with me; your rod and your staff they comfort me.

Psalm 23:4 KJV

Blessed be God, even the Father of our Lord Jesus Christ, the Father of mercies, and the God of all comfort; who comforts us in all our tribulation, that we may be able to comfort them which are in any trouble, by the comfort where with we ourselves are comforted of God.

2 Corinthians 1:3-4 KJV

Most assuredly, I say to you, that you will weep and lament, but the world will rejoice; and you will be sorrowful, but your sorrow shall be turned into joy.

John 16:20 NKJV

God shall wipe away all tears from their eyes; and there shall be no more death, neither sorrow, nor crying, neither shall there be any more pain: for the former things are passed away... Behold, I make all things new.

Revelation 21:4-5 KJV

Know therefore that the Lord your God is God; he is the faithful God, keeping his covenant of love to a thousand generations of those who love him and keep his commands.

Deuteronomy 7:9 NIV

The Lord your God is a merciful God; he will not abandon or destroy you or forget the covenant with your forefathers, which he confirmed to them by oath.

Deuteronomy 4:31 NIV

For if we believe that Jesus died and rose again, even so them also which sleep in Jesus will God bring with him. For this we say unto you by the word of the Lord, that we which are alive and remain unto the coming of the Lord shall not prevent them which are asleep.

1 Thessalonians 4:14-15 KJV

God Still Needs Me

No one needs me. I have no one to care for. How can I contribute to others?

Warn them that are unruly, comfort the feeble-minded, support the weak, be patient toward all men. See that none render evil for evil unto any man: but ever follow that which is good, both among yourselves, and to all men. Rejoice evermore. Pray without ceasing. In every thing give thanks: for this is the will of God in Christ Jesus concerning you.

1 Thessalonians 5:14-18 KJV

This is my commandment, that you love one another, as I have loved you. Greater love has no man than this, that a man lay down his life for his friends.

John 15:12-13 KJV

Whatsoever you do in word or deed, do all in the name of the Lord Jesus, giving thanks to God and the Father by him.

Colossians 3:17 KJV

God Takes Away My Bitterness
I feel that I have been overlooked and rejected. How can I overcome my bitterness?

I am come that they might have life, and that they might have it more abundantly.

John 10:10b KJV

Whatsoever things are true, whatsoever things are honest, whatsoever things are just, whatsoever things are pure, whatsoever things are lovely, whatsoever things are of good report; if there be any virtue, and if there be any praise, think on these things...And the God of peace shall be with you.

Philippians 4:89 KJV

God is able to make all grace abound to you, so that in all things at all times, having all that you need, you will abound in every good work.

2 Corinthians 9:8 NIV

Trust in him at all times; you people, pour out your heart before him: God is a refuge for us.

Psalm 62:8 KJV

Do not return evil for evil or reviling for reviling; but on the contrary bless, for to this you have been called, that you may obtain a blessing.

1 Peter 3:9 RSV

Stop your anger! Turn off your wrath. Don't fret and worry—it only leads to harm. For the wicked shall be destroyed, but those who trust the Lord shall be given every blessing.

Psalm 37:8-9 TLB

Do not say, "I'll pay you back for this wrong!" Wait for the Lord, and he will deliver you.

Proverbs 20:22 NIV

Be kind one to another, tenderhearted, forgiving one another, even as God for Christ's sake has forgiven you.

Ephesians 4:32 KJV

This is my commandment, that you love one another as I have loved you. No one has greater love than this, to lay down one's life for one's friends. You are my friends if you do what I command you.

John 15:12-14 NRSV

God Rebuilds My Burned Bridges

In some of my relationships I have built barriers instead of bridges. Is there any way I can overcome this and reach out to others?

Let love be genuine, hate what is evil, hold fast to what is good; love one another with brotherly affection; outdo one another in showing honor. Rejoice with those who rejoice, weep with those who weep. Live in harmony with one another; do not be haughty.

Romans 12:9-10, 15-16 KJV

Live in harmony with one another; be sympathetic, love as brothers, be compassionate and humble. Do not repay evil with evil or insult with insult, but with blessing, because to this you were called so that you may inherit a blessing.

1 Peter 3:8-9 NIV

This is how we know what love is: Christ gave his life for us. We too, then, ought to give our lives for our brothers!

1 John 3:16 TEV

Put on then, as God's chosen ones, holy and beloved, compassion, kindness, lowliness, meekness, and patience, forbearing one another and, if one has a complaint against another, forgiving each other; as the Lord has forgiven you, so you also must forgive.

Colossians 3:12-13 RSV

Above all, love each other deeply, because love covers over a multitude of sins.

1 Peter 4:8 NIV

My prayer for you is that you will overflow more and more with love for others, and at the same time keep on growing in spiritual knowledge and insight, for I want you always to see clearly the difference between right and wrong, and to be inwardly clean, no one being able to criticize you from now until our Lord returns. May you always be doing those good, kind things which show that you are a child of God, for this will bring much praise and glory to the Lord.

Philippians 1:9-11 TLB

All of you be subject one to another, and be clothed with humility; for God resists the proud, and gives grace to the humble. Humble yourselves therefore under the mighty hand of God, that he may exalt in due time.

1 Peter 5:5-6 KJV

Hope of Heaven

God Guarantees Eternal Life
God Overcomes My Fear of Dying
God Will Carry Me Through Death
Heaven Will Be Heavenly

God Guarantees Eternal Life

*When I think about death, it seems so final.
How can I know that I have eternal life?*

God so loved the world that he gave his only
begotten Son, that whosoever believes in him
should not perish, but have everlasting life.

John 3:16 KJV

God has given to us eternal life, this life is in his
Son. He that has the Son has life; and he that
has not the Son of God has not life. These
things have I written unto you that believe on
the name of the Son of God: that you may
know that you have eternal life, and that you
may believe on the name of the Son of God.

1 John 5:11-13 KJV

It is God himself who makes us, together with you, sure of our life in union with Christ; it is God himself who has set us apart, who has placed his mark of ownership upon us, and who has given us the Holy Spirit in our hearts as the guarantees of all that he has in store for us.

2 Corinthians 1:21-22 TEV

Not by works of righteousness which we have done, but according to his mercy he saved us, by the washing of regeneration, and renewing of the Holy Spirit; which he shed on us abundantly through Jesus Christ our Savior; that being justified by his grace, we should be made heirs according to the hope of eternal life.

Titus 3:5-7 KJV

The thief comes only to steal and kill and destroy; I have come that they may have life, and have it to the full.

John 10:10 NIV

When Christ, who is our life, shall appear, then shall you also appear with him in glory.

Colossians 3:3 KJV

God Overcomes My Fear of Dying

Even though I know I'll go to be with the Lord, sometimes I am afraid of dying. Can God relieve my fears about death?

He too shared in their humanity so that by his death he might destroy him who holds the power of death—that is, the devil—and free those who all their lives were held in slavery by their fear of death.

Hebrews 2:14-15 NIV

I sought the Lord, and he heard me, and delivered me from all my fears.

Psalm 34:4 KJV

For as in Adam all died, even so in Christ shall all be made alive...The last enemy that shall be destroyed is death...But thanks be to God, who gives us the victory through our Lord Jesus Christ.

1 Corinthians 15:22, 26, 57 KJV

He will swallow up death in victory; and the Lord God will wipe away tears from off all the faces; and the rebuke of the people shall he take away from off all the earth: for the Lord has spoken it.

Isaiah 25:8 KJV

I will ransom them from the power of the grave; I will redeem them from death. Where, O death, are your plagues? Where, O grave, is your destruction?

Hosea 13:14 NIV

God Will Carry Me Through Death

When I think about dying, I feel lonely. Will God be with me when I die?

Yes, even though I walk through the valley of the shadow of death, I will fear no evil: for you are with me; your rod and your staff, they comfort me.

Psalm 23:4 KJV

For such is God, our God forever and ever; he will guide us until death.

Psalm 48:14 NASB

I am persuaded, that neither death, nor life, nor angels, nor principalities, nor powers, nor things present, nor things to come, nor height, nor depth, nor any other creature, shall be able to separate us from the love of God, which is in Christ Jesus our Lord.

Romans 8:38-39 KJV

He will never abandon his people. They will be
kept safe forever.

Psalm 37:28 TLB

God will redeem my soul from the power of the
grave: for he shall receive me.

Psalm 49:15 KJV

Nevertheless I am continually with you; you
hold my right hand. You guide me with your
counsel, and afterward you will receive me with
honor.

Psalm 73:23-24 NRSV

Heaven Will Be Heavenly
I'm looking forward to heaven.
What will it be like?

In my Father's house are many mansions: if it
were not so, I would have told you. I go to pre-
pare a place for you.

John 14:2 KJV

The city has no need of sun or moon to shine upon it, for the glory of God is its light, and its lamp is the Lamb.

Revelation 21:23 RSV

To him that overcomes will I give to eat of the tree of life, which is in the midst of the paradise of God.

Revelation 2:7 KJV

Now there is in store for me the crown of righteousness, which the Lord, the righteous Judge, will award to me on that day—not only to me, but also to all who have longed for his appearing.

2 Timothy 4:8 NIV

I saw a new heaven and a new earth...And I heard a great voice out of heaven saying, Behold, the tabernacle of God is with men, and he will dwell with them, and they shall be his people, and God himself shall be with them, and be their God.

Revelation 21:1,3 KJV

God shall wipe away all tears from their eyes; and there shall be no more death, neither sorrow, nor crying, neither shall there be any more pain: for the former things are passed away... Behold I make all things new.

Revelation 21:4-5 KJV

PRAYERS & PROMISES

PRAYERS & PROMISES